Chess Rules of Thumb

by International Grandmaster Lev Alburt & Al Lawrence

Published by:

Chess Information and Research Center
P.O. Box 534, Gracie Station, New York, NY 10028
Telephone: 212.794.8706

For ordering information, please see page 192.

Distribution to the book trade by:
W.W. Norton, 500 Fifth Avenue, New York, NY

Staff:

Editing & Design	OutExcel! Corporation
	Email: OutExcel@aol.com
Art Director	Jami L. Anson
Editorial Consultants	Gary Colvin
	Regina DelCid
	Peter Kurzdorfer
	Daphne Lawrence
	Frank Niro
Cover Design	Jami L. Anson
Illustrations	Nicoletta Mazzesi
Photo Credits	Jami L. Anson
	U.S. Chess Federation

ISBN: 1-889323-10-1
Library of Congress Catalog Card Number: 2003098048

10 9 8 7 6 5 4 3 2 1

Printed in Canada.

Table of Contents
Chess Rules of Thumb

Introduction

Rules of thumb are general rules, rules that are correct much of the time. They're great time savers, whatever the topic. In chess, they sum up the principles of winning play. And, at their best, they can be memorable and fun.

Aaron Nimzovich, the great chess writer from the last century, was good at making them—#56, "The passed pawn is a criminal that must be kept under lock and key," is one of his. Stephan Gerzadowicz, from this century (although some would dispute it), is good as well—#223, "Defend a pawn with another pawn and get on with your life," bears the touch of his practical wit. In this book of the best chess rules of thumb from the greatest players and teachers from countries around the world and three centuries, you'll find many rules that will become your favorites.

For the most part, the rules are given in no particular order. This effect is intentional, so that your reading or sampling presents you with surprises and keeps you interested. Occasionally, we've linked or grouped some rules. Some particularly quotable and prolific rule-makers are given their own brief sections.

For those of you who would like to refer to the rules

by subject, we've supplied a subject index on page 184.

Contrary rules are given when there is valuable truth in both. You'll find some:

#21: Take a patzer into the endgame
#30: Don't trade pieces with a patzer

And we shouldn't forget to mention #41:
Violate rules for a good reason.

We identify the rule-giver when we felt we knew for sure who first said or first widely popularized a principle. Many rules have many parents, and even more rules have become part of general chess folklore.

And we'd like you to be listed as a contributor. Send us your favorite chess rule of thumb, whether you've heard it, read it, or created it yourself. If we use it in the next edition, we'll give you credit.

Please send your submissions to:

AlforChess@aol.com

Lev Alburt
Al Lawrence
New York City, October 21, 2003

Chess Notation

You don't need a chessboard to read this book. And it will seldom use any printed chess moves. But to read the moves of a game, chess players around the world use a system of "notation," a universal system for reading and writing chess. It's easy to learn, and once you know it, you'll be able to decipher any book or article on chess. The vertical columns of squares that run up and down the board are called *files* and are lettered. The horizontal rows of squares that run sideways are called *ranks* and they are numbered. The intersection of a file and a rank gives a square its name. Let's look at a board on which every square's address is given.

a8	b8	c8	d8	e8	f8	g8	h8
a7	b7	c7	d7	e7	f7	g7	h7
a6	b6	c6	d6	e6	f6	g6	h6
a5	b5	c5	d5	e5	f5	g5	h5
a4	b4	c4	d4	e4	f4	g4	h4
a3	b3	c3	d3	e3	f3	g3	h3
a2	b2	c2	d2	e2	f2	g2	h2
a1	b1	c1	d1	e1	f1	g1	h1

To make writing and reading fast, each piece is assigned a single letter. In English, we use these:

King = K	**Bishop = B**	**Rook = R**
Queen = Q	**Knight = N**	

We normally don't mention the pawn, just the square it moves to. For more on chess notation, see *The Comprehensive Chess Course, Volume 1.*

#1
Castle when you will

Castle when you will, or if you
must, but not when you can.
–John Collins

#2
Castle when you can

But for beginners: Castle when you can—unless
there is a good reason not to.   *–Lev Alburt*

#3
Control the center

Control of the center confers the possibility of
influencing activity on both wings at the
same time.   *–Aaron Nimzovich*

#4

Match plans with position

The plan must be in keeping with the character of the position.

–Wilhelm Steinitz

Wilhelm Steinitz, the first official world champion.

#5

Re-evaluate after exchanges

Any exchange requires re-evaluation of the game. This rule is especially true after the exchange of queens or non-identical pieces (for example, bishop for knight).

#6
Put pawns on e4 and d4

Try to place your pawns next to each other in the
center (d4 and e4 for White).

#7
Connect your rooks

Your development is not complete until the rooks
are connected.

#8
The endgame favors
an aggressive king

White has doubled his rooks on the c-file to win a pawn.

#9
Double your rooks

Unite the efforts of your two rooks in an important direction.

#10
Three diagonals are worth a pawn

Three useful diagonals—one for your queen and one for each of your bishops—are worth a pawn.
–John Collins

#11

A passed pawn's value increases

A passed pawn's power increases as the number of pieces on the board diminishes. *–José Raúl Capablanca*

#12

Keep knights off the eight worst squares

The eight worst squares for the knights are the four corners of the board, as well as g2, g7— and especially b2 and b7.

Lighted bombs mark the eight worst squares for the knights.

#13
Feint left, go right

Tie your opponent down on one side of
the board and then break through on the other.
–John Collins

#14
Exploit temporary advantages immediately

When we're better developed and our
pieces more active, we must exploit
such temporary advantages at once.

–Alexander Kotov

#15
No center, no defense

If the defender is forced to give up the center,
then every possible attack follows almost of itself.
–*Siegbert Tarrasch*

#16
Keep your head when studying openings

To study opening variations without
reference to the strategic concepts
that develop from them in the
middlegame is, in effect,
to separate the head
from the body.
–*Tigran Petrosian*

#17
Refute by returning

Often the best way to refute a sacrifice
lies in a well-timed return of the material.

#18
Beware the
counterattack

After an attack has been
repulsed, the counterattack
is generally decisive.

–Richard Reti

#19
Eliminate defenders

Exchange pieces that defend your opponent's weaknesses.

#20
Exchange off attackers

Exchange pieces that threaten your king.

#21
Take a patzer into the endgame

But see also Rule #30.

#22
Give it back to win

The judicious return of extra material
is the mark of the master.
–Folke Eckstrom

#23
Put two pawns
on the 4th

In the opening, try to put two pawns
abreast on the fourth rank.
–Sunil Weeramantry

#24
Attack on the side
you have more space

#25
Your king is only as weak as your opponent's ability to attack it

–Sunil Weeramantry

#26
Accumulate advantages

Winning a game is a matter of accumulating advantages.

#27
You control your destiny

#28
Play where your strength is

#29
Visualize what is left
on the board after
the trade

#30
Don't trade pieces
with a patzer

#31
Take your time in an unfamiliar situation

#32
Don't chase the knight to a better central square

Do not chase a knight with a center pawn if the knight can go safely to a better central square.

#33
Learn where pieces belong

Learn the "normal" positions for pieces
in the openings you play.

White has congested his development with a badly placed piece.

#34
Don't block your central pawns

The same is true for c-pawns when 1. e4 e5 has not been played.

#35
Prioritize

Don't overvalue small points at the expense of more serious concerns (for example, material).

#36
Seize the initiative

#37
Play the isolani like a gambit

When you find yourself with an *isolani*, think of it as playing a gambit, but without the material commitment!

White has an *isolani* in this position in the Queen's Gambit (after 12. Ne5!)

#38

Don't trade off your enemy's problems

Avoid trades and other moves that free
your opponent's pieces or give him more space.

#39

Plant a knight in front of your opponent's isolani

The square in front of an isolated pawn
is an ideal post for an enemy knight.

#40

Even the first move counts

An unenterprising move such as 1. c3?! would reduce
the game to immediate equality. Even worse is 1. f3?.

#41

Violate rules for
a good reason

#42

Become discriminating

Learn to appreciate even small differences.

#43
GM Whites are 3-5-2

For every ten GM games played nowadays,
White wins three, draws five and loses two.

#44

Think space

Think about space advantages, both
in general and in specific areas of the
board—on the queenside, center and
kingside. *–Bruce Pandolfini*

#45
Drive enemy pieces from your territory

#46
Analyze forcing lines first

#47
In the endgame, a knight is weaker than three pawns

In the ending, a knight (but not a bishop)
is often weaker than three pawns.

#48

Use candidate moves

When it's your move, make a mental list of candidate moves—the likely, logical choices in the position.

#49

Use your first impression

After selecting several candidate moves, make a quick, superficial review of them. Perhaps one will appear to be the most promising, or you'll discover some other candidate moves, or candidate variations.

#50
Always make a judgment

Considering variations, always make a judgment and conclude with an evaluation, even if it's "The position is unclear; further calculation is required."

#51
Trust your home analysis

However, there are exceptions, as sometimes external pressure can unleash your creativity.

#52
You can accept a weakness in return for active play

#53

Those who live behind an isolani should not cast the first trade

... the chess commandment for those with an isolated pawn—don't trade pieces without a good reason. After all, in the endgame, the *isolani* becomes simply a weak pawn. (But see #205.)

#54

Castle early and castle often

(After Chicago mayor Richard Daley's "Vote early and vote often.")

#55

The purpose of the opening is to get to a playable middlegame

Keep in mind that tiny theoretical plusses have no meaning in games between non-titled players.

#56

Imprison passed pawns

The passed pawn is a criminal that must be kept under lock and key.

–Aaron Nimzovich

#57

Rooks belong behind passed pawns

Let your rook "push" your passed pawn!

... whether it's your pawn or your opponent's!
–*Siegbert Tarrasch*

This rule is especially true for endings with one rook for each player.

#58

When analyzing, don't jump aimlessly back and forth

Analyze each line—a candidate move and its possible consequences—and conclude with an evaluation before going to another candidate move.

#59
Stop the passer

A passed pawn must be captured by pieces, or blocked, or else it will eventually be promoted.

–Emanuel Lasker

#60
Trade off the enemy's fianchettoed bishop

Often you can trade your bishop of the same color for your opponent's *fianchettoed* bishop.

White forces a trade of Black's *fianchettoed* bishop on g7.

#61
Beware of stereotypical thinking!

#62
Don't sell your advantages too cheaply

#63
In closed positions, think big picture

In closed games, your plans should be based on broad strategic considerations.

#64
You don't have to be perfect to win

Sometimes slight inaccuracies do not allow the victim to escape.

#65
Material, like money, isn't everything

Material alone can't be relied on as an absolute indicator in every situation. But, like money, you can generally take it to the bank.

#66
When you analyze, shift perspective
–Bruce Pandolfini

#67
In difficult situations, make practical decisions

#68
Try to answer threats by combining defense with counterattack

#69
Once you've reached an endgame, don't automatically castle

–Bruce Pandolfini

#70
Tactics flow from a superior position

–Bobby Fischer

#71

In a quiet ending, you can try to hatch a long-term plan

#72

Rooks love open files

However, not all open files are created equal.

#73
Learn to play with an isolani

The *isolani* represents one of the most important middlegame structures in the whole of chess.

#74
The opening's connected to the ending

The Benko Gambit is an excellent illustration of how openings should be studied—in close connection, not only with the middlegame, but also with the endgame.

#75

Don't mimic; understand

In studying openings, try to understand why so-called "theoretical" moves are supposed to be good.

#76

The judicious violation of basic principles marks the master's mind

–Folke Ekstrom

#77

In endings with bishops of opposite color, pawns are expendable

White (2 pawns down) draws by sacrificing a third: 1. c5! Bxc5 2. Bb3! (targeting). Forcing the e6-pawn to move to a dark square, White builds an impregnable fortress.

In endings with bishops of opposite color, pawns are sacrificed even more freely than in rook endings.

#78

Knight endings are like pawn endings

Knight endings are governed by the rules similar to those of pawn endings. For example, an outside passer is a clear plus.

#79
Rook pawns are a knightmare

The knight is ill-equipped to stop a far-advanced rook pawn.

#80
1. e4! Best by test

—Bobby Fischer

Bobby Fischer (left) and Boris Spassky shake hands in 1972.

#81
Develop your pieces quickly

#82
Develop a different piece on each move

#83
Find a good square for your piece and leave it there

#84
Develop your pieces so they are in harmony

#85
In the endgame, centralize your king

In the early endgame, keep your king close to the central files; in the late endgame, march it toward the center of the board.

#86
Don't retreat pieces to the first rank

#87
Value of the king— negative to plus three

The value of a king as a fighting piece changes during the course of a game. It's at first negative, then turns to a plus (in most endings). In the late ending, it equals approximately three pawns.

Now White should NOT play 3. d3, but move the bishop outside of his pawn-chain with 3. Bb5 or 3. Bc4.

#88
Develop bishops outside of your pawn-chain

#89
KNP+1 =70%

In a knight-and-pawn endgame, with four pawns versus three pawns on the same side of the board, the extra pawn wins 70% of the time.

#90
Beware the poisoned pawn
Never capture the b2 pawn with the queen.

#91
Knights belong in the center of the board

#92
Don't bring out the queen too early
Unless it's for a good reason.

#93

In queen endings, pawn quality is worth more than pawn quantity

In such endings, having an advanced passed pawn is more important than having more pawns.

#94

Endgame mastery separates the men from the boys

#95

In the endgame, don't think in terms of moves, but in terms of plans

–*José Raúl Capablanca*

José Raúl Capablanca

#96

Learn the endgame from the greatest

Study Capablanca, Rubinstein, Smyslov and Karpov. Analyze their games—with *their* annotations.

#97

In pawn endings, the more the merrier

This is true only for the side with the extra pawn(s).

#98

Beginner's piece values: 10-5-3

(Q=10 pawns, R=5 pawns, B or N=3 pawns)

Why is the queen stronger than three minor pieces? Perhaps it's due to the queen's psychological omni-importance for beginners.

#99
Expert's piece values: 9-5-3.5-3.25

(Q=9 pawns, R=5 pawns, B=3.5 pawns, N=3.25 pawns)

#100
Rooks love endings

Rooks benefit more than any other piece from going into the ending.

#101

Piece values change

The values of the pieces are different
in the middlegame and the endgame.

In the middlegame:
Two bishops are worth more than a rook and two
pawns. Bishop and knight are worth slightly
more than a rook plus two pawns. Two knights
are worth less than a rook and two pawns.

In the endgame:
Two bishops are worth more than a rook and
two pawns (still!). Bishop and knight are worth
more than a rook plus *one* pawn. Two knights
are worth less than a rook and a pawn.

#102

Pawns blossom in the endgame

The value of a pawn increases the most when going into an endgame. The pawn's increase in value is even greater than that of the rook!

#103

With a rook against two minor pieces, exchange queens

If you have a rook against bishop and knight or against two knights, exchanging queens equals winning a full pawn.

Black has just played 3. ... c5!, attacking White's pawn-chain at its base.

#104

Attack a pawn-chain at its base

#105

Don't launch premature attacks

#106
Knights on the side cannot abide

#107
When you see two unprotected pieces, try to fork them

#108
Exchange your redundant rook

If you have two rooks versus a rook and a minor piece (or two minor pieces), exchange your "redundant" rook for your opponent's only rook.

–*Mikhail Botvinnik*

It doesn't matter who is better, nor how many pawns each side has. Exception: Two extremely well coordinated rooks, like Nimzo's "blind pigs" on the 7th rank (see rule #125).

#109
Don't trade pieces when you're behind in material

#110
Non-redundant piece-pairs are stronger

The less redundant two pieces
are, the stronger they are
in combination.

–Mark Dvoretsky

For example, queen-plus-knight is stronger than
queen-plus-bishop—but rook-plus-knight is weaker
than rook-plus-bishop. And, of course, the bishop pair
is never redundant, because your two bishops never
control the same squares.

#111
Trade pawns when you are behind in material

So, combining #109 and #111: when behind
in material, trade pawns not pieces.

1. ... f5!! 2. e5 c4!
Gligorich–Smyslov, 1959

#112
Keep your pawns next to each other

The center becomes fixed, and thanks to his being able to force White to play e4-e5, Black will own the important d5-square. He can then safely build up his queen-side advantage.

#113
The queen doesn't fear two rooks–unless she's alone

In the opening and the early middlegame, a queen is at least equal to two rooks. With no other pieces left, two rooks are stronger by almost a full pawn.

#114

Capture toward the center

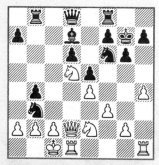

Exception: Here it's safer for White to capture with the c-pawn.

Important exception: in pawn endings and knight endings, take toward the edge of the board because *outside passed* pawns are the strongest.

Take away from the center only for this and other compelling (and concrete) reasons.

For instance, in the diagram (Sax–Bilek, 1975), White's king is safer after capturing with the c- (rather than with the a-) pawn. Still, when in doubt, follow the rule!

#115
Queens love checks and loose change

When fighting other pieces, a queen is at its strongest when the opponent's king is open to checks (thus giving the queen extra mobility) and when there are some loose pieces and pawns.

#116
With no checks, the queen is weaker

When there are no checks available, and no weaknesses, rook-bishop-and-pawn are stronger than a queen.

#117

A passed pawn has a lust to expand

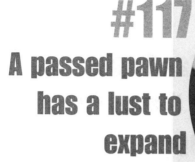

—Aaron Nimzovich

#118

Three goals of the opening: center, development and castling

For White, emphasis is on the first two.
Black should emphasize the third (king's safety).
Thus, Black usually castles short.

#119

When you stand better and can use the d-file —castle long

This is more often the case for White.

#120

Answer an attack on the flank with a counterattack in the center

#121

When the opponents have castled on opposite sides, he who gets there first wins

When attacking in a position with opposite-side castling, an initiative and an open file against the opponent's king are worth at least a pawn.

#122

In a race to get the opponent's king, material is of less importance than time

These "dim" knights have no good moves. The knight on a1 will be lost after 1. Kb2.

#123
A knight on the rim is dim

The great 19th-century German grandmaster and writer, Dr. Siegbert Tarrasch, said "Das Pferd am Rande ist immer Schande." In English, this literally translates as "The knight on the rim is a shame." But we prefer to keep Tarrasch's rhyming format.

#124
Two bishops and a pawn equal a rook plus knight

This is the modern evaluation–compare #129.

#125
Rooks united on the seventh are blind pigs

Nimzovich called a pair of rooks on the opponent's second rank "blind pigs" because they devour everything indiscriminately.

#126
Attack a knight on Knight 6 (b6, g6) with your rook pawn

#127

A knight secure on the fifth can be worth a rook

The knight on the fifth rank, supported by a pawn, with no pawn to drive it away and no minor piece to exchange it, is stronger than a bishop and nearly equal to a rook (when on central squares or close to the opponent's king).

#128

A knight on the sixth rank is even stronger

#129

The bishop pair may be worth rook plus knight

–Siegbert Tarrasch
Compare #124.

#130

The bishop pair keeps its value

The bishop pair is of the same high value
in all stages of the game.

#131

Every chess player should have his own opening secrets

#132
Last rounds are never won

#132-#134
Tigran Petrosian

#133
It's easier to win an equal rather than a worse position

#134
White is always equal; Black is always worse

When I analyze an opening for White, it's always equal. When I analyze for Black, it's always worse.

#135
Recognize five characteristics of a critical position

1. When the game changes from known theory into unknown territory, from opening to middlegame, or from middlegame to endgame.
2. When any pieces are exchanged, especially queens.
3. When there is any change, or possible change in the pawn structure—especially in the center.
4. When you have a tactical (short-lived) advantage which will disappear if not exploited now.
5. When you see a move which seems to win.

#136
A critical position is one about which you should think long and hard

#137
Buy a steak for your opponent

"I'll buy a steak for my opponent—if he agrees to eat it no more than two hours before our game starts."   *—Walter Browne*

Yes, during the game we need blood going into the brain, not the stomach. That's why black caviar (small volume, lots of calories, plus a lot of phosphorus—see rule 325!) was a preferred lunch of many Soviet prodigies. During later hours of the game, eat chocolate: again, a small burden for your stomach, but many calories—plus some caffeine!

#138
Play the position you have right now

Don't wish for an earlier chance. Don't blame yourself, don't pity yourself and, importantly, don't look for excuses.

#139

Don't blunder because of a blunder

When you see your last move was a blunder, first calm down. Even go to get a drink (tea, coffee, water) and perhaps some fresh air. Then try to evaluate objectively the new situation on the board. Remember, a new mistake often follows on the heels of an earlier one.

#140

Rehearse

Prepare yourself in advance for various game and tournament contingencies. Plan how you'll behave when leading in a tournament. How will you act if you get a poor start? How about if your opponent blunders? Or what if you lose a game you think you should have won?

#141
Know how to stay cool

How will you react to surprises during your games?
Prepare techniques for "calming down," for boosting
your self-confidence. (Recall, for instance, your victo-
ries over opponents stronger than the current one, or—
after a serious blunder—your Houdini-like escapes.)

#142
Don't trade pieces when you have the initiative

#143
Trade pieces in cramped positions

#144
Trade pieces when you're under attack

#145
Attack with at least three pieces

But don't miss 2. ... Qh4 checkmate after 1. f4 e6 2. g4.

#146
Don't imitate your opponent's moves without good reason

#147
Don't get your king trapped in the center

#148
Block the center before attacking on the wing

#149
If your opponent attacks your castled king, break open the center

#150
Attack on the side your pawns are pointing to

#151
The king is a powerful piece in the endgame—use it

#152
Don't gamble

Don't make an unsound combination hoping
your opponent doesn't see the refutation.

#153
Doubled pawns
may be bad

... but not as often
as many people think.

**Black has doubled pawns,
but his two bishops and the
semi-open d-file provide
compensation.**

#154
Avoid pawn islands

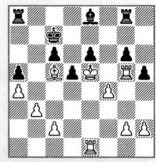

Black's three pawn islands allow White to infiltrate with 1. Kf6!, winning. (Bernstein—Mieses, 1904)

#155
Think carefully before changing pawn structure, or opening or closing the game

Such moves can determine the entire future course of the game.

#156
Knight's dream square is d5

#157
When you fianchetto, try to trade off your opponent's bishop of that color

But don't use your own bishop for this!

ANDRE DANICAN PHILIDOR
geb. zu Dreux d. 7 Sept.
CIƆIƆCCXXVI.

#158
Pieces belong behind pawns

—André Philidor

#159

Time pressure is the enemy of cognizance

–Al Lawrence

#160

When your opponent is in time trouble, play strong rather than quick

In time pressure, we make natural-looking moves. Try to create situations for your opponent where such a move would be an error.

#161
Sicilian endgames favor Black

Because Black usually has play
over the semi-open c-file.

#162
Alekhine endgames favor Black

In the opening and middlegame, the far-advanced
e5-pawn restrains Black forces and often allows
White to launch an attack; in the ending,
it becomes a weakness.

#163
Pawns can't move backward So be sure you want to move them!

#164
All rook endings are drawn
—Savielly Tartakower

When down a pawn or even two, going into a
rook-ending is usually the best defense.

#165
Patzer sees check;
Patzer gives check

#166
Sacrifice your
opponent's pieces
—Savielly Tartakower

#167
Give your opponent chances to go wrong

#168
You never win a game by resigning

#169
Don't trade a developed piece for an undeveloped one

#170
Pile on a pinned piece

White wins with 1. Rxc5!!
Rxc5 2. Rc2 Rfc8 3. Qb5!!
Rxc2 4. Bxa7 Rxa2 5. Bc5
h6 6. h4 Kh7 7. h5.
(Kotov-Kholmov, 1971)

#171
A pinned piece provides little protection

White wins with 1. Nxc5+;
Black can't recapture.

#172
Don't move the pawns in front of your king needlessly
–Genna Sosonko

#173
Knights are better than bishops in blocked positions

#174
Bishops are better than knights in open positions

#175
Rooks belong on the seventh rank

#176
A weak back rank invites deflection

#177
Don't be a pawn grabber

#178
Passed pawns are meant to distract

And the farther the opponent's king is from the passed pawn, the stronger its power to distract.

#179
Without pawns, you must be a rook ahead to win

There are exceptions: two rooks win against two minor pieces; two bishops win against a knight; four minor pieces win against a queen.

#180
When two or more pawns ahead in the ending, advance your pawns

It's a routine win!

#181
With only a pawn advantage, use it to gain more material

#182
The key piece to many of White's attacks is his king's bishop

#183
The weakest square in Black's camp before castling is f7

"Scholar's Mate" follows with 1. Qxf7, checkmate.

#184

The weakest square in Black's camp after castling is h7

White wins with 1. Rxe6!
Qxd5 (if 1. ... fxe6 2. Qg6) 2.
Rxh6!+ Kg8 3. Rh8+ Kxh8
4. Qh3+ Kg8 5. Qh7 mate.
(Udovic—Bertok, 1954)

#185

Play better players

Give a man a fish and he can eat one meal.
Teach a man to fish and he can feed himself
for the rest of his life. But give a man a fish to play
chess with and he may never learn anything again.

–Al Lawrence

#186

Answer two questions before each move

1. How does the move affect the center?
2. How does the move fit in with the development of my other pieces and pawns?

#187

To offer a pawn in the opening, there must be one of four reasons

1. Secure tangible advantage in development.
2. Deflect the enemy queen.
3. Prevent the enemy from castling, either permanently or for several moves.
4. Build up a strong attack.

#188

Chess is a game of understanding, not memory

–Eugene Znosko-Borovsky

#189

Place bishops on open diagonals

#190

Stifle counterplay

#191
In a rook-and-pawn endgame, an active rook is worth a pawn

Here you can see both tactics. Black, on move, wins with 1. ... Rd3+ and 2. ... Rxe3.

#192
The two most common tactics are double-attacks and pins

#193

Don't put pawns on the same color as your bishop

#194

Keep your pawns together

#195

Position comes first; material next

#196
Take every pawn or piece you can unless you see immediate danger

#197
Learn the two sides of the isolani

An isolated d-pawn can be a powerful attacking platform in the middlegame, but a grave weakness in the endgame.

#198
The goal of the ending is to queen a pawn

#199
Don't push pawns on the side you're weaker

—Mark Dvoretsky

#200
When you have the bishop pair, open the game

#201

Don't play for cheapos unless you're hopelessly lost

"Cheapos" are second-best moves that give your opponent a chance to go horribly wrong, but also give him a chance to punish you.

#202

Isolate a sick buffalo

Identify your opponent's worst piece (the "buffalo") and consider how to restrict its abilities even further.

—Sam Palatnik

Sam Palatnik and wife Olga after accepting the 2003 Frank J. Marshall award

#203

If you have no center, your opponent has a freer position

–Siegbert Tarrasch

#204

If you do have a center, then you really have something to worry about

Chess is a terrible game.

–Siegbert Tarrasch

Siegbert Tarrasch
#205-#211

#205

Between the opening and the ending the gods have placed the middlegame

#206

If one piece stands badly, your whole game is bad

#207

Sit on your hands

#208

When you don't know what to play

... wait for an idea to come into your opponent's mind. You may be sure that the idea will be wrong.

#209

A cramped position contains within it the germs of defeat

Concise diagnosis by Doctor Siegbert Tarrasch.

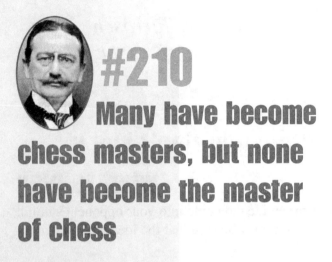

#210
Many have become chess masters, but none have become the master of chess

#211
First-class players lose to second-class players

... because second-class players sometimes play a first-class game.

#212

Holes in the opponent's position must be occupied by pieces, not pawns

#213

Even a poor plan is better than no plan at all

#214
It is not enough to be a good player ... you must also play well

#215

Discovered check is the dive-bomber of the chessboard
–Reuben Fine

#216
Chess is 99% tactics
–Rudolf Teichmann

#217
Play the opening like a book, the middlegame like a magician, and the endgame like a machine *–Rudolf Spielmann*

Marcy and Andy Soltis

#218
Chess is really 99% calculation
–Andy Soltis

#219

In open positions, calculate

When the game is "open," with lots of open files and diagonals, you should strive to calculate as many concrete variations and sub-variations as practical.

#220

Rely on your intuition

... and on your subjective discrimination.
Your conclusions may not be perfect,
but you will be developing good chess habits
and proper analytical skills.

#221
Choose chess books that offer more words than moves

Games that are annotated purely with symbols, without any accompanying text, tend to confuse the average player. Symbols do indicate who stands better, but the essential elements that contributed to the assessment are left to the hapless student to deduce for himself.

#222
When you see a good move, wait ... look for a better one

–Emanuel Lasker

Lasker, seated on far right

Stephan Gerzadowicz
#223-#227

Stephan (second from right) with the 2003 National Blind Chess Championship Participants

#223 Defend a pawn with another pawn–and get on with your life

#224

Beware of three situations

Mistakes are most often made when, in inverse order,
(1) exchanging pieces; (2) pushing pawns; and
(3) exchanging pawns.

#225 Push a pawn, burn a bridge

Stephan Gerzadowicz
#223-#227

#226

An extra pawn is nice, but you have to survive to enjoy it

Stephan (back row, fourth from right) stands with the 2003 Denker Championship Participants along with GM Arnold Denker, GM Susan Polgar, Jack Mallory, John McCrary and Dewain Barber.

#227

If you're not sure what to move, move a piece not a pawn

If it doesn't turn out such a red-hot idea, you may be able to repair the damage with a discreet retreat.

#228
Find a plan ...
don't just make moves

#229
Cash in toward the center

Except in the endgame:
Central pawns are worth $1.
Bishop pawns = $.90
Knight pawns = $.80
Rook pawns = $.70

–Fred Reinfeld

Sometimes, as in the
Sicilian, you can
"exchange and keep
the change"!

–Al Lawrence

**Fred Reinfeld
in center**

#230
Resist automatic moves

Be sure to think before making "natural" moves, such as recaptures and checks, so that you are alert to other possibilities.

#231
Not all pawns are created equal

Note how White's pawn majority leads to a passed pawn; Black's doesn't. Many such "Ruy" endgames are won for White, especially king-and-pawn and knight endgames.

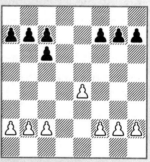

This pawn structure would win for White in the endgame.

#232
When a pawn down, leave pawns on one side only

#233
Remember to look backward

Many mistakes overlook the fact that diagonally moving pieces can move backward! The mistake is especially easy to make when there are a lot of squares between the enemy's bishop or queen and your piece.

–Bent Larsen

#234
An extra pawn equals 50% winning chances

#235
General principles are important, but tactics have the final say

#236

Those who rely on chance should play cards or roulette; chess is something quite different

–Tigran Petrosian

#237

Some part of a mistake is always correct

–Savielly Tartakower

#238
The game is a draw theoretically

–Bobby Fischer

#239
Pawn endings are the irreducible wins, losses and draws of chess

They are the atoms of chess physics, the foundation of endgame play.
–Lev Alburt

#240 Pawns are the soul of chess

–André Philidor

#241

Snap off the buttons and the pants fall by themselves

–Samuel Reshevsky

Another comment on the importance of pawns.

#242

Every pawn is a potential queen

–James Mason

#243
Opening surprises don't win games by themselves

It is usually not enough to surprise your opponent with an opening innovation, even one that is rock-solid. You must continue to play well afterwards. And, in order to win, you may still need a degree of "cooperation" from your opponent.

–Lev Alburt

#244
Ask yourself questions

When playing or analyzing, ask yourself questions. The thoughts of a master during a game are, indeed, chiefly a discussion of such questions.

Savielly Tartakower
#245-#250

#245

Sacrifices only prove that someone has blundered

#246

I've never defeated a healthy opponent

#247

Castling is the best way to an ordered life

Savielly Tartakower
#245-#250

#248

The most important moment of the game is the first bishop move

#249

All the mistakes are there on the board, waiting to be made

#250

The gambit in chess: "eat while you can"

#251
The winner is the one who commits the next-to-last mistake

#252
Know when to calculate

Knowing *when* to calculate is just as important as knowing *how* to calculate.

–Sam Palatnik

#253
Take a risk and you might lose; never take a risk and you'll always lose
–*Savielly Tartakower*

Left to right: Akiba Rubinstein, Edmond Landau, Edgar Colle, and Savielly Tartakower

#254
Pin it and win it

#255
Rook endings are never easy
–C.J.S. Purdy

#256

Half the variations calculated in a game turn out to be superfluous
–Jan Timman

Unfortunately, no one knows in advance which half.

#257
Know how to play the minority attack

The purpose of the minority attack is to create weaknesses in the opposing pawn structure that will negate the value of having a majority of pawns on that wing. This theme is a common one in chess. Learn how to play it and defend against it.

#258
Queen and knight are better than queen and bishop

Especially with no other pieces left on the board, the queen and knight work better in tandem than the queen and bishop duo. It so happens that the knight's unique and versatile movement better complements the queen's long-range striking power.

#259

A rook on the seventh is worth a pawn

–Reuben Fine

#260

Chess is not a crap game

Too few amateurs are aware that playing for a win does not necessarily mean venturing risky gambit lines or super-sharp attacks. As the Russian psychologist GM Nikolay Krogius advises, "You must not allow your ambition to win to turn chess into a game of chance."

#261

Every chess master was once a beginner –*Irving Chernev*

#262

Black must equalize first

Even when playing for a win, Black's objective
in the opening is first to reach an equal position and
only then to try to gain an advantage. It's possible
to outplay an opponent from an equal position, so
long as dynamic possibilities exist for both sides.
So, to win as Black, avoid variations that simplify too
quickly, that exchange off many pieces, or that create
symmetrical pawn structures.

#263
One bad move nullifies forty good ones
—Al Horowitz

Al Horowitz (standing) studies a move

#264
Take a deep breath after turning down a draw

Sometimes when a player refuses a draw, he unconsciously tries to justify his decision with a move more aggressive than is needed. At times, you can even offer a draw with this possible effect in mind!

#265
Trade rooks warily

Don't trade rooks just for the sake of simplicity–
especially if it gives away an open file.

#266
Everybody blunders, even grandmasters

–Bent Larsen

José Raúl Capablanca
#267-#270

#267

You learn more from a game you lose than from a game you win

You will have to lose hundreds of games before becoming a good player.

#268

Chess books should be used as we use glasses

Use them to assist the sight, although some players make use of them as if they thought they conferred sight.

José Raúl Capablanca
#267-#270

#269

If you think the move is good, play it

#270

Study the endgame first

To improve your game, you must study the
endgame before everything else, for the endings
can be studied and mastered by themselves.
The middlegame and the opening must
be studied in relation to the endgame.

#271
Learn from mistakes
... your own–as well as your opponents'.
Your goal is not to repeat them.

#272
A good player
is always lucky

#273

Conduct the attack so that when the fire is out ... it isn't
–Reuben Fine

#274

The farther the better

In bishops-of-opposite-color endings (with bishop plus two pawns vs. lonely bishop), if you cannot touch both your pawns with the out-stretched fingers of one hand, you'll win.

–Vladimir Simagin

#275

All that matters on the chessboard is good moves

Bobby Fischer with chess teacher John Collins

–Bobby Fischer

#276

The pin is mightier than the sword

–Fred Reinfeld

#277 Don't give up

When in a lost position, continuously present your opponent with problems.

#278

In blitz, the knight is stronger than the bishop —*Vlastimil Hort*

#279

Rook-pawn endings are drawn

Only the prudent 1. g3! wins here.

#280

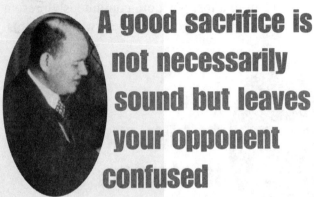

A good sacrifice is not necessarily sound but leaves your opponent confused

–Rudolph Spielmann

#281

Threats are the basis for winning chess

–C.J.S. Purdy

#282

Time management is an important skill in chess

Having 15 minutes left when your opponent has five is worth about 200 rating points!

–Dan Heisman

#283

Any opening that you know well is good no matter what its reputation

–Dan Heisman

#284

The first principle of attack is: Don't let the opponent develop

–Reuben Fine

#285

Count the pieces on the board

Don't rely solely on counting captured men.

–Leon Balmazi (in a Soviet instructional manual)

#286
Gambits are a leg up

The root word for gambit is *gamba*, leg. Picture a wrestler with a leg just a little extended. Should the opponent go for it? Now a good leg hold could give considerable advantage. But is that what he wants you to do? Grabbing a leg puts you a little off-balance, out of position. He might drop you with a better hold of his own. Ah, but if you get a good lock on that leg!
–*Stephan Gerzadowicz*

#287
Decide for yourself what to remember and what to forget

Aaron Nimzovich
#288-#291

#288

The isolated pawn casts gloom over the entire chessboard

#289

The defensive power of a pinned piece is only imaginary

Aaron Nimzovich
#288-#291

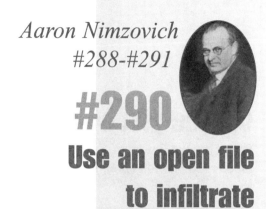

#290

Use an open file
to infiltrate

The aim of all maneuvers on an open file is the ulti-
mate intrusion along this file onto the seventh or
eighth rank, i.e., into the enemy position.

#291

Even the laziest king flees
wildly in the face of
a double check!

#292

Cut the piece off

Reducing the power of a single enemy piece may provide enough advantage to win the game.

–Sam Palatnik

#293

Thou shalt not shilly-shally

–Aaron Nimzovich

#294

To mobilize a pawn majority, push the unopposed pawn first

–José Raúl Capablanca

#295
Study patterns and look for them as you play

Learning patterns will provide you with a variety of tools, which you would be able to successfully apply in various chess struggles.

#296
The threat is stronger than the execution

–Aaron Nimzovich

#297
Don't take a draw out of relief

Sometimes when improving from a lost to an unclear position, a player will accept a draw too readily. Actually, he should take advantage of his new psychological edge. But never relax too soon—that is, any time before your opponent stops his clock and resigns!

#298

Best defense: pawns on f7, g6 and h5

In the diagram, if White is to move, 1. g4! gives him some (approximately 30%) chance of winning. Otherwise, Black will play … h7-h5 and cut White's chances in half.

In an endgame with pawns on only one side of the board, to create a passer, White will be forced to exchange too many pawns to achieve real winning prospects.

Get the knights into action
before both bishops are
developed

When you see a
good move, try
to find a better one

Emanuel Lasker
#301-#304

#301

Good players can play bad positions

Everybody can play well in better positions, but to be a good player it is necessary to also play well in bad positions.

#302

Reason governs also the chessboard

Emanuel Lasker
#301-#304

#303

Distrust opening theory

Show me three lines of the opening theory
moves and I will prove to you that two
of them are incorrect.

#304

No combination without
a big plus; no big plus
without a combination

#305
Know when to look for winning combinations

The chess player should not look for winning combinations, unless he can prove to himself that he has the advantage.

#306
The hardest game to win is a won game

#307
Keep on fighting as long as your opponent can make a mistake

#308
Create a hook

Force your opponent's pawns to advance on the side where you'll attack. Then use them as a "hook" on which to hang your attack.

#309

A lone bishop (or knight) usually draws against a lone rook

There are many positions with bishop and pawn, and some with knight and pawn, that draw rook and pawn. There are also positions in which bishop and two pawns draw against rook and two pawns. There are even positions where bishop and three pawns can draw against rook and three pawns!

#310

To conquer a file, take control of the back square

–Eugene Ruban

#311

With rooks or queens on the board, watch out for a weak back rank

Black wins with 1. ... Qb2!,
highlighting White's
back-rank weakness.
(Bernstein—Capablanca, 1914)

Some Statistics

#312

20% of bishop-of-opposite-color endings with one extra pawn are won

#313

60% of bishop-of-opposite-color endings with two extra pawns are won

Some Statistics

#314
80% of king-and-two-pawns vs. king-and-one-pawn endgames are won

#315
90% of king-and-three-pawns vs. king-and-two-pawns endgames are won

#316

Hierarchy of winnable endings: King-and-pawn, knights, queens, bishops, bishop vs. knight, knight vs. bishop, four rooks, two rooks, bishops of opposite color

King-and-pawn endings are the most winnable.
Bishops-of-opposite-color endings
are the least winnable.

#317

The stronger side of a rook-bishop-and-pawn ending should not trade bishops

With a pawn ahead, about 50% of rook-bishop-and-pawn endings are won–but only about 40% of rook-and-pawn endings are won.

#318

Don't blitz in the opening

Unless you frequently find yourself in time pressure (and then analyzing how you're spending your time will help), you probably make the same mistake as most non-professionals–you play too fast in the opening.

1. Rxc7+ looks attractive. But reversing the order with 1. Qa7+ mates in three.

#319

To go forward, think in reverse

If you're having trouble making a combination work, reversing the move order often works wonders.
–Lev Alburt

#320

Reinforce important squares

For instance, a square in front of your opponent's isolated passed pawn.

#321

Don't overburden your bishop

Try to confine your bishop's important functions to a single diagonal.

#322

Think along the top

… of the variations. Before you go into a jungle of deep variations, search for different opportunities for yourself, and for your opponent, on the very first moves.

#323

The endgame has its own rules

Of the three phases of the game—opening, middlegame and endgame—the endgame has the least in common with its fellow stages in terms of principles guiding correct play. In fact, some rules good in the opening and middlegame reverse themselves in the endgame!

#324

In response to an opening surprise, think three minutes plus half the time you saved on previous moves

The first critical moment in the game occurs when your opponent makes a new move—a move after which you're not 100% sure what to play. It's very tempting—and very wrong—to keep playing fast.

My advice: On average, spend on your next move your "normal" three minutes plus half of the time you've saved on trusted, "known" moves.

–Lev Alburt

Mikhail Botvinnik
#325-#326

#325

Conserve your phosphorus

Don't have sex within three days of a tournament game! Botvinnik, a decorated scientist and doctor's son, felt that male players should refrain from sex before a game, because the act robbed the body of phosphorus, an element crucial to brain processes. (Movie fans may be somewhat reminded of the fictional General Jack D. Ripper's anxiety about preserving his "bodily fluids" in Stanley Kubrick's 1964 film, *Dr. Strangelove.*)

#326

Walk before a game

Botvinnik maintained that a 40-50 minute walk stored oxygen in your brain. He felt a familiar and pleasant route was best.

Grandmaster's Corner

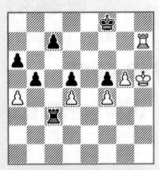

A possible variation from
Capablanca—Tartakower,
New York, 1924.
After 37. ... b5

After 42. Rf6

#327

Beware opening files adjacent to passed pawns

—Isaac Efremovich Boleslavsky

GM Igor Zaitsev writes in the Russian magazine *64* that "Once in the mid-eighties, analyzing the Ruy, Boleslavsky dropped this phrase that I then found quite mysterious."

In the top diagram, what possible difference could it make if White plays Kh5-g6 with or without exchanging on b5?

In fact, including the exchange appears more appealing—it saves White the time needed to consider 38. Kg6 bxa4 (White wins here, however).

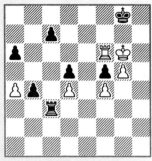

With the a-pawns, Rxa6 wins.

But after the hasty 38. axb5 axb5 39. Kg6 Kg8! 40. Rg7+ Kf8 41. Rf7+ Kg8 42. Rf6 (see second diagram on page 156), Black holds with the simple 42. ... b4, e.g. 43. Ra6 Ra3! (grabbing the file!) 44. Rc6 Rc3, and it's equal. Put the a-pawns back on the board and this defense obviously doesn't work (and neither does any other). Thus, Black should look for other methods to counter 38. Kg6—but all those fail, too.

#328

Discover and learn rules of thumb

Try to discover and learn new chess paradigms. They'll improve your game more than most opening novelties. –*Igor Zaitsev*

Zaitsev's upcoming book will discuss exactly this type of "axiomatic knowledge."

The pawn will queen, even if it's Black's move

#329

King-and-pawn endings are for squares

Rule of the Square: Imagine an equal-sided box drawn from the pawn's current square to its promotion square. Draw the square toward the king. If the king is within the square (or on move can get into the square) he can catch the pawn. If he can't, he'll lose the race and the game. When the pawn is in its starting position, be careful to take into account its first-move option of leaping forward two squares.

Black to move. The king catches the pawn.

This time-saving aid to calculation was invented in the 19th century by the Austrian player and writer Johann Berger. The Rule of the Square always works, assuming the king is unobstructed from his shortest path.

#330

Squares can be movers

Rule of the Moving Square: If the joint square of two pawns (divided by two files) reaches the 8th rank, one of them will queen; otherwise, the King will capture them, one by one.

In the diagram above, after 1. h5, the joint square reaches the 8th rank, and White wins. If Black is to move, 1. ... Kg6 wins. With White's pawn still on e4 (see the second diagram), the joint square reached only 7th rank. Black wins, no matter who is to move.

#331

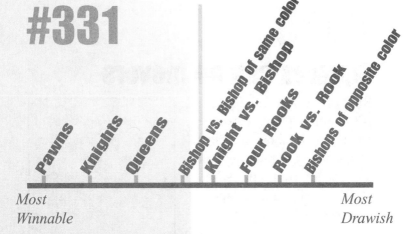

Pawns · Knights · Queens · Bishop vs. Bishop of same color · Knight vs. Bishop · Four Rooks · Rook vs. Rook · Bishops of opposite color

Most
Winnable

Most
Drawish

In knight endings, an extra pawn often wins. In rook endings, two extra pawns win, while one extra pawn wins less than 50% of the time.

#332
Never buy a chess book that's not fun

Guide to the Openings

Chess literature is filled with the names players have for certain openings, names like "Queen's Gambit," "Ruy Lopez," "Sicilian" and "Danish Gambit." The following 10 pages give you the defining moves of the 40 key openings.

It's good to keep in mind that it takes both players to make an opening. Whether you're playing White or Black, your opponent will usually have as much to say about what opening you wind up playing as you do.

Openings have "personalities." The Caro-Kann is known for being placid while the King's Gambit is known for its kamikaze tendencies. But many openings have split personalities. The French can be stolid or wild, depending on the further choices the opponents make.

Some openings are "shortcuts" because they avoid the most heavily-analyzed paths. For any tournament chess player with a job and a lawn to mow, these debuts can be a godsend.

In keeping with our rules-of-thumb approach, we've summed up each opening's general persona in a few lines.

Openings

Albin Counter-Gambit
1. d4 d5 2. c4 e5 3. dxe5 d4

An impatient attempt by Black to wrest the initiative on the second move! White can get an edge.

Alekhine's Defense
1. e4 Nf6

Very provocative and original. Black tempts White to overextend his center in order to destroy it.

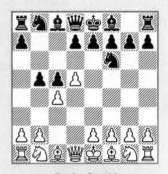

Benko Gambit
1. d4 Nf6 2. c4 c5 3. d5 b5

Black offers a solid, strategic pawn sacrifice. An opening that plans on a good ending!

Benoni Defense
1. d4 Nf6 2. c4 c5

Father of many openings, the Benoni creates unbalanced, fighting games.

Blackmar-Diemer Gambit
1. d4 d5 2. e4

A favorite of a cabal of attacking specialists. It quickly opens lines, but Black should equalize.

Bogo-Indian Defense
1. d4 Nf6 2. c4 e6 3. Nf3 Bb4+

A solid reply to solid 3. Nf3. Black has developed his kingside pieces and is ready to castle.

Budapest Gambit
1. d4 Nf6 2. c4 e5

For the defender who wants to attack! Sharp and risky, but certainly playable.

Catalan Opening
1. d4 Nf6 2. c4 e6 3. g3 d5

A positional choice for White, pressuring the long diagonal, the center and queenside.

Openings

Caro-Kann Defense
1. e4 c6

Ultra-solid, conservative defense against 1. e4. Prepares 2. ... d5 without blocking the queen bishop.

Center Game
1. e4 e5 2. d4 exd4 3. Qxd4

Exposing the queen too early, it is rarely played nowadays. Black equalizes with 3. ... Nc6.

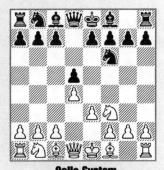

Colle System
1. d4 d5 2. Nf3 Nf6 3. e3

Simple and easy to learn, it's been called the "busy man's opening." It plays for mate or a good ending.

Danish Gambit
1. e4 e5 2. d4 exd4 3. c3 dxc3
4. Bc4 exb2 5. Bxb2

Swashbuckling play puts White ahead in development, but Black will equalize with ... d5.

Dutch Defense
1. d4 f5

Morphy's choice and a crusty survivor! Its main idea is to prevent White's e2-e4. Cp. the Sicilian.

English Opening
1. c4

Generally a subtle approach, and a close relative of 1. d4. It can transpose into many openings.

Evans' Gambit
1. e4 e5 2. Nf3 Nc6
3. Bc4 Bc5 4. b4

For Whites of the attacking kind. You'll get compensation for your pawn.

Four Knights' Game
1. e4 e5 2. Nf3 Nc6 3. Nc3 Nf6

Old and solid, it's considered somewhat dull, but contains a drop of poison.

Openings

French Defense
1. e4 e6 2. d4 d5

A solid form of counterattack for Black against 1. e4. The defense Fischer had the most trouble with!

Giuoco Piano
1. e4 e5 2. Nf3 Nc6 3. Bc4 Bc5

The "quiet game" is not so "giuoco" in some lines. The granddaddy of the open game.

Gruenfeld Defense
1. d4 Nf6 2. c4 g6 3. Nc3 d5

Combines the strategic and tactical. Black yields White a big center—in order to counterattack it.

King's Gambit
1. e4 e5 2. f4

This macho opening is still alive, thanks to modern attackers like Spassky, Bronstein and J. Polgar.

King's Indian Defense
1. d4 Nf6 2. c4 g6 3. Nc3 Bg7

A sharp, dynamic defense. Allows White to build a big center in return for quick development.

Larsen's Opening
1. b3

Like GM Bent Larsen, offbeat and dangerous. It can start out as a quiet buildup but end in a mate!

Latvian Gambit
1. e4 e5 2. Nf3 f5

This gambit is a bit similar to sword-swallowing. It may impress, but will likely lead to injuries.

Nimzo-Indian Defense
1. d4 Nf6 2. c4 e6 3. Nc3 Bb4

Solid and strategic. In modern fashion, Black doesn't occupy the center, but exerts pressure on it.

167

Openings

Petroff's Defense
1. e4 e5 2. Nf3 Nf6

A solid "shortcut" which eliminates the bookwork necessary to playing 2. ... Nc6.

Philidor's Defense
1. e4 e5 2. Nf3 d6

Solid but passive. An opening analyzed 300 years ago, but still played today.

Pirc Defense
1. e4 d6 2. d4 Nf6

Resilient and provocative. Black plans to fianchetto his black bishop and to pressure White's center.

Polish (Orangutan) Opening
1. b4

Played by specialists to get Black out of his comfort zone of knowledge. Reasonable moves equalize.

Queen's Gambit Accepted
1. d4 d5 2. c4 dxc4

Played today at the top, it normally leads to isolani-based attacks or subtle endgames.

Queen's Gambit Declined
1. d4 d5 2. c4 e6

Classic defense to 1. d4. This "Orthodox" setup with e6 blocks the QB but frees the KB. Cp. French.

Queen's Indian Defense
1. d4 Nf6 2. c4 e6 3. Nf3 b6

A solid, positional reply after 3. Nf3, a less forceful move than 3. Nc3. Cp. the Bogo-Indian.

Reti Opening
1. Nf3 d5 2. c4

Positional and slippery, can transpose into other closed openings, such as the Queen's Gambit.

Openings

Ruy Lopez
1. e4 e5 2. Nf3 Nc6 3. Bb5

A rich mine of sharp tactics and deep strategies, it was once the right of passage for the master.

Scandinavian (Center Counter) Defense 1. e4 d5

Black plays the "equalizing" thrust ... d5 immediately! Once reviled, now considered okay.

Scotch Game 1. e4 e5 2. Nf3 Nc6 3. d4 exd4 4. Nxd4

An alternative to the Ruy Lopez brought back from history by Kasparov.

Sicilian Defense
1. e4 c5

Brings Black the most wins against 1. e4! The idea—watch the center and take on d4 with the less valuable c-pawn.

Slav Defense
1. d4 d5 2. c4 c6

Solid, popular defense. This setup with c6 frees the QB but delays freeing the KB. Cp. Caro-Kann.

Two Knights' Defense
1. e4 e5 2. Nf3 Nc6 3. Bc4 Nf6

A contemporary of the Giuoco Piano, it is likewise overanalyzed. Full of pitfalls for the unwary.

Veresov Opening
1. d4 d5 2. Nc3 Nf6 3. Bg5

A "shortcut" that saves White from learning extensive theory after 2. c4. Chiefly strategic.

Vienna Game
1. e4 e5 2. Nc3

Solid but unenterprising 19th-century favorite—still dangerous in the hands of a devotee.

Glossary

Absolute pin: A piece or pawn that is pinned to the king is absolutely pinned. Moving the piece or pawn off the pinning line is not possible, since this would expose the king to check.

Action chess: Chess played at a time control of thirty minutes per game per person.

Adjust: A player, when it is his turn to move, may adjust (slide a chessman to the center of the square) pieces by first announcing "j'adoube" or "I adjust".

Algebraic notation: A method of recording moves in which each square is named for its intersecting rank (1 through 8) and file (a through h). Nd4 means that the knight (N) has just moved to the fourth rank of the queen's (d) file.

Attack: Various ways to try breaking down your opponent's defense.

Back-rank mate: A checkmate delivered by a queen or rook against a king located on his first rank.

Backward pawn: A pawn whose neighboring pawns have been pushed forward. Backward pawns may be weak due to lack of protection by other pawns.

Battery: Any two long-range pieces of the same color lined up along one line of attack.

Black: The dark pieces are referred to as Black in chess, regardless of their actual color. The player handling the Black pieces is also referred to as Black.

Blindfold chess: A game of chess that is played by one or both opponents without sight of a board and pieces.

Bishop: A piece that moves on diagonals, any numbers of squares, and starts out next to the king and queen. Each player gets two; one that travels on light-square diagonals, one that travels on dark-square diagonals. It was originally an elephant.

Bishops of opposite color: A situation where each opponent has a bishop, one controlling the light squares and the other controlling the dark squares.

Blitz chess: Chess played at a very fast time control–normally five minutes per player per game (a.k.a. speed chess).

Blunder: A very unfortunate move.

Book: Within known opening theory. A move can be "book" or "out of book"–not part of theory.

Breakthrough: Creating a far-advanced passed pawn with a sacrifice.

Building a bridge: An endgame technique in which a rook creates a shelter for a king in order to promote a pawn without enduring endless checks from the enemy rook.

Caissa: The mythological goddess of chess.

Candidate moves: The set of moves under consideration at any given time during a game.

Capture: A pawn or piece may be captured (removed from the board) when an opponent's piece or pawn moves to the square the captured pawn or piece occupied, replacing it.

Castling: A player moves the king two squares to the right or left toward one of his rooks. The rook is then moved to the opposite side of the king and placed on the adjacent square. Neither piece may have moved before, the squares between king and rook must be empty, and the king may not castle into, out of, or through check.

Center: The squares e4, d4, e5, and d5 comprise the geometrical center of the board. It is important to fight for control of the center of the board. Central development allows for greater mobility and space for the pieces.

Check: A move that places the king under attack is a check.

Checkmate: When one king is under attack and there is no legal way to get the king out of check, it is called checkmate.

Chess board: A checkered board with 64 alternately light and dark squares in an eight by eight arrangement.

Chess clock: A device with two clocks connected to keep track of each individual's time during a chess game.

Chess computer: A computer dedicated solely to playing chess.

Closed file: A file occupied by pawns of both colors.

Closed game: The type of game that naturally develops from pawns being blocked in the center. Usually arises from the moves 1. d4 d5.

Combination: A series of moves with a central theme or idea that involves a sacrifice, combining tactical weapons to gain some advantage.

Consolidation: The process of coordinating and/or trading pieces in order to stabilize one's position.

Computer chess: Chess played by or analyzed by a computer program or chess computer.

Corresponding squares: An endgame situation in which certain squares are linked to other squares. When the enemy king goes to one square, your king must be able to get to its corresponding square.

Decoy: The tactic of forcing your opponent to go to an unfavorable square.

Defense: Various ways to hold back or neutralize your opponent's threats.

Deflection: Coaxing a defending piece away from its post.

Descriptive notation: An archaic system of recording the moves where each square has two names, depending on each player's point of view.

Desperado: A tactic in which a piece or pawn that is lost in any case captures an enemy piece or pawn to take along with it or sacrifice itself to achieve a stalemate. See Kamikaze.

Development: Moving the pieces from their starting squares, usually towards the center of the board.

Diagonal: A slanted row of squares of the same color running either from corner to corner or from one side of the board to the adjacent side.

Discovered attack: A surprise attack created when one piece (or pawn) moves and uncovers an attack by another piece on the same rank, file, or diagonal.

Discovered check: A type of discovered attack that places the king in check.

Discovery: See Discovered Attack.

Distant passed pawn: A passed pawn far away from other pawns.

Double (or multiple) attack: A tactic which threatens two or more enemy men simultaneously.

Double check: A discovered check that puts the king in check from two different directions. The only way out is to move the king.

Doubled pawns: Two friendly pawns occupying the same file. Doubled pawns are often weak, since they cannot protect each other.

Doubled rooks: Two friendly rooks occupying the same rank or file (a.k.a. battery).

Draw: A tie game. No one wins, no one loses.

Draw by perpetual check: A draw resulting when one player checks another *ad infinitum*.

Draw by repetition: A draw resulting from repeating the same position three (not necessarily consecutive) times.

Dubious move: A move that is intuitively considered doubtful, but is not proven to be bad.

Elo system: The currently used system of rating chess players, named for its co-developer, Arpad Elo (1903-1990), an American statistician born in Hungary. American Kenneth Harkness also deserves credit.

E-mail chess: Chess played via e-mail.

Endgame: The stage of the game in which so many pieces have been captured that the kings can take an active part in the battle and passed pawns assume extra importance.

En passant: This is a French term that means "in passing." When one player moves a pawn two squares forward to try to escape capture by the opponent's pawn, the pawn is captured in passing as though it had only moved one square forward.

En prise: A French term meaning "in take." A piece is *en prise* when it is under attack and undefended.

Exchange (the): Generally, any trade of pieces or pawns; "The queens were exchanged." Specifically, a term for the trading of a rook for a minor piece; winning a rook for a bishop or a knight is called "winning the Exchange."

Exclam: A slang term used by chess players to indicate a very good move –written as an exclamation point in all chess notation.

Fianchetto: The development of the bishop to b2, g2, b7, or g7.

Fifty-move rule: The game is drawn after 50 moves without any capture or pawn move.

File: A vertical row of squares running between the two opponents. These rows are named by the letters "a" through "h."

Fish: Slang for a very weak player, particularly one who plays for money.

Fixed pawns: Pawns that cannot move because the squares in front of them are occupied.

Flank opening: An opening featuring a *fianchettoed* bishop.

Flight square: Any square to which a piece can safely flee (a.k.a. escape square).

Fool's mate: The shortest game ending in checkmate (two moves). For example: 1. g4 e5 2. f3 Qh4 mate.

Forfeit: The loss of a game due to overstepping the time limit or a penalty imposed by the tournament director.

Fork: All pieces and pawns are capable of forking. This special tactic occurs when a single piece or pawn attacks two or more of the opponent's pieces and/or pawns.

Gambit: A material sacrifice in the opening (usually a pawn) in exchange for some kind of advantage.

Half-open file: A file that has a pawn of only one color on it is half-open; the side without a pawn has a half-open file.

Hanging: See *En prise*.

Horizon effect: A weakness in the play of chess computers, caused by an inflexibility in their search methods. When facing inevitable material loss, a computer might unnecessarily weaken its position or sacrifice material to push the loss beyond its "search horizon" (the number of moves ahead the computer is able to see).

Initiative: The ability to call the shots (the attacking player has the initiative).

Interference: A tactic used to disrupt the interaction of your opponent's forces.

Internet chess: Chess played over the Internet. There are many servers that allow such play, including the ICC (Internet Chess Club).

Isolated Pawn: A pawn with no other friendly pawns on the files adjacent to it. These tend to be weak since they cannot be protected by other pawns.

J'adoube: French for "I adjust." A player, when it is his turn to move, may adjust (slide a chessman to the center of the square) pieces by first announcing "j'adoube" or "I adjust." (See Touch move).

Kamikaze: See *Desperado*.

Kibitzer: A pesky individual who comments on games in progress, offering players a wealth of unsolicited and often useless advice.

King: The most important piece in a chess game. When the king is trapped (this is called checkmate), the game is over, with the side that trapped his opponent's king victorious.

King safety: Since he is the whole game, it makes sense to keep your king safe behind a wall of pawns until the danger of checkmate is much reduced.

Kingside: The half of the board from the e-file to the h-file, where the kings originate.

Knight: Shaped like a horse's head, this chess piece leaps over all adjacent squares to a different colored square. Each player gets two knights, and they begin the game between the bishops and the rooks. Originally cavalry, or mounted warriors.

Knight's tour: A puzzle whose object is to move a knight to every square of an empty board, visiting each square only once.

LCD: Liquid Crystal Display; that which enables you to see information on your computer via the screen.

Line clearance: A rank, file or diagonal is cleared out when a piece or pawn moves off of it. See Discovered Attack.

Long-range pieces: Queens, rooks, and bishops. These are pieces that can cover an entire open line in one move.

Looking ahead: Visualizing a new position after one or more potential moves without actually moving the pieces.

Lucena position: An endgame theme employed to protect a king from rook checks, using a technique that is called "building a bridge."

Luft: German for "air." Luft signifies the creation of a future flight square for the king, in order to avoid a back-rank mate.

Major pieces: The rooks and queen; the pieces that have the potential for controlling the most squares.

Mate: Short for checkmate.

Middlegame: The second of three phases of a chess game, the point at which development has been completed, but few captures have taken place.

Minor pieces: The bishops and knights; these pieces generally control fewer squares than the queen and rook.

N: Symbol representing a knight, since K represents the king.

No retreat: A situation in which a piece has nowhere safe to go.

Notation: A system for recording the moves of a chess game.

Open file: A file that has no pawns on it.

Opening: The first of three phases of a chess game. Basic opening strategy consists of development, control of the center, and castling into safety.

Opposition: A technique used to force the opponent's king to move away by placing your king with one square between him and the opponent's king on a rank or file with the opponent to move.

OTB: Over the board (generally used as opposed to postal or correspondence chess).

Overload: The state of a piece having too many functions at once.

Overprotection: The protection of a key piece or pawn or square by more pieces and pawns than are immediately necessary.

Parting with the lady: Slang for sacrificing the queen.

Passed Pawn: A pawn with no opposing pawns on the files adjacent to it, which enables it to advance unmolested by enemy pawns.

Patzer: Slang for a very weak player (similar to fish).

Pawns: The little guys that line up in front of the pieces at the start of a game. Pawns have always been the foot soldiers of chess, and each player starts out with eight.

Pawn chain: Diagonally adjacent pawns of the same color.

Pawn grabber: A chess player who snatches material with dangerous disregard for the consequences.

Pawn promotion: When a White pawn reaches the eighth rank or a Black pawn reaches the first rank, it has the option of becoming a queen, rook, bishop, or knight. It cannot promote to a king or fail to promote.

Pawn skeleton: The configuration of the pawns.

Pawn storm: An attack on the enemy position by several connected pawns.

Pawn structure: Refers to the placement of pawns in any given position.

Philidor's position: A famous rook vs. rook-and-pawn draw.

Pieces: Kings, queens, rooks, bishops, and knights are the pieces in chess.

Pin: A tactic that "sticks" or "pins down" one piece to another along a rank, file, or diagonal. The pinned piece is always less valuable than the piece it is pinned to. Only a long-range piece can execute a pin.

Ply: One half of a move pair; a single move for White or Black.

Positional: Concerned with a game's long-term effects, as opposed to tactics.

Postal chess: Chess by mail (a.k.a. correspondence chess.)

Postmortem: The analysis that takes place after a game.

Pre-chess: A variation of chess in which the pieces are placed on the back ranks in any order the player chooses. Placing the pieces constitutes the first eight moves.

Provisional rating: An unofficial estimated rating based on the results of less than 20 tournament games.

Pup: Slang for perpetual check (a.k.a. "purp").

Queen: Originally the king's counselor, this chess piece grew tremendously in strength during the Renaissance. Each player gets only one. She can move in any straight line, along ranks, files, or diagonals, any number of unobstructed squares.

Queenside: The half of the chessboard from the d-file to the a-file, where the queen originally resides.

Quick chess: Chess played at a time control slower than blitz chess but quicker than action chess (generally 10 to 15 minutes per player per game).

Rating: Earned from the USCF (see page 189) for participating in official tournaments. The four-digit numbering system is divided into categories every 200 points: from master (2200

and above) through expert (2000-2199) to class E (below 1200)

Rank: A row that runs from left to right across the board (numbered 1 through 8).

Removing the defender: A tactic that removes the defender of a given square, piece, or pawn, so that it is no longer defended.

Roll: A sequence of alternating checks by two pieces (usually two rooks or queen and rook) which drives the enemy king to an edge (a.k.a. lawnmower technique).

Rook: An adaptation of an old Sanskrit word for chariot (rukh), this chess piece has evolved into a ship in some countries and a tower on a castle in others, such as the United States. The rook moves along ranks or files, any number of squares, and is capable of castling with the king occasionally. It starts out in the corners when a game begins, and each player gets two.

Rule of the square: A helpful analytical tool to determine quickly whether a lone king can catch an enemy passed pawn.

Sacrifice: Giving up material to gain some other advantage. Often used for attacking the king.

Sandbagger: An inconsiderate, dishonest, and unethical player who deliberately loses games in order to lower his rating so that he might later win money in a lower section of a big tournament.

Scholar's mate: Mate delivered when the White queen, supported by a bishop, captures the pawn on f7.

Semi-open game: A game that starts 1. e4 and is answered with a move other than 1. ... e5.

Shot: An opportunity to execute a combination or a single move that will improve your position: "I missed a shot on Move 17 and lost."

Simul: Abbreviation for simultaneous exhibition (a master or expert playing against several, perhaps very many, opponents at once).

Skewer: The skewer is a backward pin. It is an attack on two pieces and/or pawns on the same rank, file or diagonal by a long-range piece. But, unlike the pin, the more valuable piece is in front, while the less valuable man is in back. If both front and back pieces (or pawns) are the same value, it is also a skewer.

Slow chess: Another name for traditional chess, often played at a time control of 30 moves in 90 minutes, followed by sudden death.

Smothered mate: A checkmate delivered by a knight in which the king is trapped on all sides by his own men and has no place to flee.

Square clearance: When a piece would gain power if only it could use a certain square, but that square is occupied by a friendly piece or pawn, an option is to clear the square for the piece that wants it by simply moving the guy that's there off the square. Naturally, if you can make a threat with the vacating piece or pawn, it will be all the better!

Stalemate: A tie game brought about by a position in which there are no legal moves for the player on move, and the player's king is not in check.

Staunton design: The standard design of chess pieces used today, offered in the U.S. by House of Staunton. To order go to: www.houseofstaunton.com

Strategy: Dealing with overall plans or goals as opposed to tactical calculations.

Sudden death: A time control in which the players have a set time to finish the game, no matter how many moves are involved.

Tactics: The fireworks of chess. These are tricks or weapons used to win material or gain some other advantage. They include batteries, pins, forks, skewers, discovered attacks, removing defenders, Zwischenzug, etc.

TD: Tournament director.

Three-D: Chess played on a three-tiered board, adding the third dimension–as if traditional chess weren't confusing enough.

Tiebreak: In the event of a tied score, a system used for deciding who wins a prize that cannot be split, such as a trophy.

Time control: A designated time allowance for a certain number of moves.

TN: Theoretical novelty; an opening move that is unfamiliar to analysts, but looks pretty good.

Touch move: In chess if you touch a piece without saying "I adjust" or "j'adoube" first, then you must move it to any legal square. Once your hand leaves the piece or pawn just moved, the move is made.

Tournament chess: An event where chess games are played among a number of players.

Triangulation: An endgame situation in which the king takes two moves to get to a square he could have gone to in one move, thus giving the appearance of tracing a triangle.

Unclear: A positional evaluation by grandmasters who don't feel like analyzing any further!

Under-promotion: Pawn promotion to a rook, bishop, or knight.

Universal notation: A method of recording moves in which pieces are designated by an actual picture of the piece itself, followed by the algebraic name for the square (a.k.a. figurine notation).

USCF: The United States Chess Federation.

WBCA: World Blitz Chess Association (the brainchild of Grandmaster Walter Browne).

White: The light pieces are referred to as White in chess, regardless of their actual color. The player handling the White pieces is also referred to as White.

Windmill attack: A combination in which a piece captures several enemy pieces via repeated discoveries on (usually) the king, which can only helplessly toggle back and forth as his army crumbles, piece by piece. The windmill usually involves a rook on its seventh rank supported by a bishop.

Winning the Exchange: If you win a rook for a bishop or a knight, you have won the Exchange.

Woodpusher: Slang for any chess player, but often used to refer to a very weak player.

X: The symbol meaning "captures" or "takes."

Zugzwang: A German word that refers to a situation in which any move will make the position worse.

Zwischenzug: A German word that means an in-between move.

Art Director
Jami Anson

Winner
of many awards
for design,
photography
and layout

Jami Anson has lent her creative hand to assist in the design and production of Lev Alburt's books. She is the winner of many Chess Journalist of America awards and the Cramer Award for best chess photography. Her photographs have appeared in magazines such as *Time Magazine* and *TV Guide*, as well as in many newspapers and books.

Jami has designed art for many firms— Sterling Publishing, McGraw Hill, Excalibur Electronics, Chess n' Bridge, ChessCafe, OutExcel Corp., Lev Alburt, Lindberg Associates and Seiko.

After 17 years of designing and producing *Chess Life* and *Schoolmates* for the U.S. Chess Federation, Jami started her own design firm—JadanDesign.

During her tenure at *Chess Life*, she maintained and built up the research libary and photos that span chess history from the early 1800s to the present day. She is currently creating a cultural center in her home town from an abandoned church called Little Apple Restoration. This project will include classes in art, music, theatre and, of course, chess.

Contact Jami Anson at:
jadandesign@aol.com

Al Lawrence

Author and co-author of 10 books on a variety of subjects, Al Lawrence has been at the center of the chess scene since the early 1980s. He's friendly with four world champions and has met and talked with several more.

Lawrence was Executive Director of the U.S. Chess Federation during a decade of innovation and record-breaking growth. A former public school and college teacher with advanced degrees in instructional techniques, he is especially interested in applying modern teaching theory to chess.

He is president of OutExcel! Corporation (Email: OutExcel@aol.com), a marketing and publishing firm. He is also Chief Executive Officer of StarFinder, Inc. (Skyfind@aol.com), which develops and patents products that make it easy for amateur stargazers to learn and enjoy the night sky. StarFinder's "Night Navigator" has been featured internationally in magazines and on television.

Lawrence was selected as "Journalist of the Year" for 2000-2001 by the Chess Journalists of America (CJA).

Lawrence is currently Executive Director of the World Chess Hall of Fame in Miami. You can reach him at ChessMuseum@aol.com.

Former USCF Executive Director

Author of ten books

- ◆ CJA Journalist of the Year 2000-2001

- ◆ *World Book Encyclopedia* contributor

- ◆ Former college and public school teacher

- ◆ Holder of advanced degrees in instructional techniques

- ◆ President of OutExcel! Corp.

- ◆ CEO of StarFinder, Inc.

- ◆ Executive Director of the World Chess Hall of Fame

Lev Alburt

GM Alburt lived for many years in Odessa, a Ukrainian city located on the Black Sea. He won the highly competitive Ukraine championship three times, from 1972-1974. He won the European Cup Championship twice, in 1976 and 1979.

In the days when there were still a Berlin wall and a tight KGB-guard on "Soviet" GMs, Alburt defected while at a tournament in what was then West Germany.

In 1979, he came to the U.S., making his home in New York City. He won the U.S. Championship an impressive three times–in 1984, 1985 and 1990.

Famous for providing aspiring players easy access to master-level ideas, Alburt is the only top-echelon GM to devote his career to teaching non-masters. *The Comprehensive Chess Course*, which he co-authored and published, is a long-time best seller.

Lev provides lessons through-the-mail, over-the-telephone, and face-to-face. Write to GM Lev Alburt at PO Box 534, Gracie Station, New York, NY, 10028, or call him at (212) 794-8706.

Alburt and Lawrence, from opposite sides of the old "Iron Curtain," have been writing partners and friends for two decades.

Renowned player, teacher and writer

Mentored by world champion & pre-eminent teacher Mikhail Botvinnik

- Three-time US Champion: 1984, 1985, 1990

- Twice US Open Champion: 1987, 1989

- Three-time Ukraine Champion: 1972-74

- Popular *Chess Life* Columnist

- Inductee in the U.S. Hall of Fame

Subject Index (numbers refer to rule numbers)

Subject index

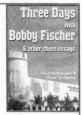

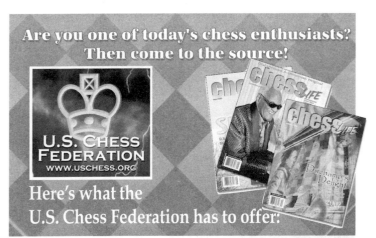

189